Delicious & Deep

Fried

The Deep Fryer Cookbook Collection

BY: Valeria Ray

License Notes

A Special Reward for Purchasing My Book!

Thank you, cherished reader, for purchasing my book and taking the time to read it. As a special reward for your decision, I would like to offer a gift of free and discounted books directly to your inbox. All you need to do is fill in the box below with your email address and name to start getting amazing offers in the comfort of your own home. You will never miss an offer because a reminder will be sent to you. Never miss a deal and get great deals without having to leave the house! Subscribe now and start saving!

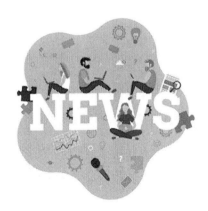

https://valeria-ray.gr8.com

Contents

Simple and Delicious Deep-Fried Recipes

ZZZZZZZZZZZZZZZZZZZZZZZZZZZZZZZZZZZZZZZZZZZZZZZZZZZZZZZZZZ

Chapter I - Fried Chicken Many Ways

There's no denying that fried chicken is everybody's favorite deep-fried treat. In fact, various food businesses capitalized on how the crunchy chick phenomenon grew and never stopped becoming big. Various fried chicken versions were also introduced so people could have an excuse for having fried chicken everyday (It's a different recipe!).

If you are a fan of fried chicken, you will love this section of this deep fryer cookbook. We will give you an insight into some of the most popular and utterly delicious fried chicken recipes.

zzzzzzzzzzzzzzzzzzzzzzzzzzzzzzzzzzzzzzzzzzzzzzzzzzzz

(1) Honey-Glazed Fried Chicken

The rich and crunchy fried chicken is this time drizzled with a delightful glaze that will truly enhance its flavors and make it taste even better. Honey is the common choice for the glaze sauce, but you can go ahead and experiment with using other ingredients. The addition of lemon or orange flavor would not hurt.

Yield: 8

Preparation Time: 40 minutes

List of Ingredients:

- 8 pcs chicken thighs and drumsticks
- 3 cups all-purpose flour
- 3 cups buttermilk
- 2 tablespoons garlic powder
- 2 tablespoons onion powder
- 3 tablespoons paprika
- 2 tablespoons dried oregano
- 2 tablespoons ground cumin
- 2 teaspoons cayenne powder
- 2 tablespoons salt
- 3 tablespoons black pepper
- Honey
- Vegetable oil for frying

zzzzzzzzzzzzzzzzzzzzzzzzzzzzzzzzzzzzzzzzzzzzzzzzzzzzzzzz

Methods:

1. Combine all the spices together with flour and coat chicken pieces.

2. Add buttermilk and toss.

3. Place in the fridge for about 2 hours or more.

4. When chicken is ready, remove it from marinade and preheat oil in the deep fryer until its temperature reaches 325 °F.

5. Before frying, dip each chicken piece into flour, into buttermilk marinade, and back to flour for extra crispiness.

6. Fry in hot oil until cooked through and golden brown or for about 12 minutes.

7. Drain on paper towels and drizzle generously with honey before serving.

(2) Chicken Nuggets

Chicken nuggets are great for parties, for kids' school snacks, and for just about any occasion. Some people just could not have enough of these crunchy, meaty nuggets so make sure to cook a good batch so you will never get short of a platter to serve your eager loved ones.

Yield: 8

Preparation Time: 45 minutes

List of Ingredients:

- 8 pcs chicken breast, skinned, deboned, and cut into chunks
- 4 pcs eggs, lightly beaten
- 4 cups all-purpose flour
- 6 tablespoons garlic salt
- 3 tablespoons ground black pepper
- Vegetable oil for frying

ZZZZZZZZZZZZZZZZZZZZZZZZZZZZZZZZZZZZZZZZZZZZZZZZZZZZ

Methods:

1. Preheat oil in the deep fryer until its temperature reaches 350 °F.

2. Mix together flour, salt, and pepper in a bowl; place beaten eggs in another.

3. Dip each chicken chunk into eggs, then coat with flour mixture.

4. Make sure to shake off excess coating before placing the nuggets to fry in hot oil.

5. Cook for about 3-5 minutes or until golden brown and cooked through.

(3) Japanese Karaage

Who says the Japanese would be left behind in a battle for the best fried chicken in the world? Their version features a rich mix of fresh spices like garlic and ginger. The thin, simple coating of flour and cornstarch is enough to keep it crispy as everyone loves their fried chicken to be. Plus, since this recipe uses boneless chicken thighs, so you get that rich texture minus the hassle.

Yield: 4

Preparation Time: 30 minutes

List of Ingredients:

- 1 lb. boneless chicken thighs, fat and skin trimmed and cut into 1-inch chunks
- 2 garlic cloves, minced
- 2 teaspoons fresh ginger, grated
- 2 tablespoons soy sauce
- ¼ cup cornstarch
- ¼ cup all-purpose flour
- Kosher salt and freshly ground pepper to taste
- 1 qt peanut oil
- 1 pc scallion, thinly sliced
- 1 pc lemon, cut into wedges

zzzzzzzzzzzzzzzzzzzzzzzzzzzzzzzzzzzzzzzzzzzzzzzzzzz

Methods:

1. Mix soy sauce, garlic, and ginger in a large bowl.

2. Add chicken and mix until meat is well coated with marinade.

3. Cover bowl and chill in the fridge for an hour or overnight.

4. When chicken is ready, preheat oil in the deep fryer until its temperature reaches 350 °F.

5. Mix together cornstarch and flour in a shallow dish.

6. Remove chicken from the marinade and coat one-by-one in cornstarch mixture, shaking off any excess.

7. Fry in hot oil until beautifully browned and cooked through or for about 5-7 minutes.

8. Drain chicken on paper towels and sprinkle with salt and pepper. Serve with lemon wedges and sliced scallions.

(4) Korean-Style Fried Chicken

We love all things Korean and it would not hurt if we learn the way they do fried chicken, too. This recipe is remarkable for its ultra-thin batter that crackles with every bite. It is super crunchy and super delicious. Let a serving of this surprise you and endear you to the K-pop culture even more.

Yield: 4

Preparation Time: 1 hour

List of Ingredients:

- 2 lbs. chicken wings, cut whole
- ½ cup vodka
- ½ cup cold water
- ½ cup all-purpose flour
- ¾ cups cornstarch
- 1 teaspoon baking powder
- 2 qt peanut oil or vegetable shortening
- 4 teaspoons Kosher salt

zzzzzzzzzzzzzzzzzzzzzzzzzzzzzzzzzzzzzzzzzzzzzzzzzzzzzzz

Methods:

1. Combine ¼ cup of cornstarch together with half a teaspoon of baking powder. Season with 2 teaspoons of salt.

2. Coat chicken wings in cornstarch mixture, making sure you coat evenly and thinly.

3. Shake off any excess before arranging chicken in a wire rack placed on top of a baking sheet. Chill for 30 minutes uncovered, or if you have time, you can do this overnight.

4. Preheat oil in the deep fryer until its temperature reaches 350 degrees F.

5. Combine remaining cornstarch with flour, 2 teaspoons salt, and ½ teaspoon baking powder.

6. Whisk in vodka and water to form a smooth, thin batter. You can add as much as 2 tablespoons more of water if the batter becomes too thick.

7. Dip each chicken piece onto the batter, shaking off excess, and deep fry into hot oil for about 8 minutes or until crisp and golden brown all over.

8. Drain on paper towels before serving it with sweet and spicy chili sauce or sweet soy sauce.

(5) Chicken and Waffles

A nice wonderful trick on serving fried chicken differently is serving it on top of buttermilk waffles, complete with some thick, rich syrup. When these two amazing meals come together in one delightful serving, the result could be life-changing. Brace yourself for the oohs and aahs that you will be getting from your loved ones.

Yield: 4

Preparation Time: 55 minutes

List of Ingredients:

- 4 buttermilk waffles
- 8 pcs chicken wings
- 2 cups buttermilk
- 2 ½ cups all-purpose flour
- 4 tablespoons cornstarch
- 2 teaspoons worcestershire
- 2 teaspoons hot sauce
- 1 tablespoon onion powder
- 2 teaspoons paprika
- 3 tablespoons seasoned salt
- 1 teaspoon garlic salt
- 2 teaspoons freshly ground black pepper
- Vegetable oil
- Confectioner's sugar
- Maple syrup

zzzzzzzzzzzzzzzzzzzzzzzzzzzzzzzzzzzzzzzzzzzzzzzzzzzzzzz

Methods:

1. Place chicken in a Ziploc bag together with buttermilk, Worcestershire sauce, and hot sauce. Toss to coat and allow to marinate in the fridge for at least two hours.

2. When chicken is ready, preheat oil in the deep fryer until the temperature reaches 325 °F.

3. Combine flour, cornstarch, onion powder, salt, pepper, and paprika in a bowl.

4. Add two tablespoons of chicken marinade into the flour mixture and stir until crumbly.

5. Fry chicken wings until golden brown.

6. Drain on paper towels.

7. Assemble the dish by placing a chunk of butter on buttermilk waffles, top with fried chicken wings, drizzle with maple syrup, and sprinkle with confectioner's sugar.

(6) Fried Chicken Sandwich

Fried chicken is best enjoyed with a side serving of either rice, mashed potatoes, or stir-fried veggies. But if you are a burger person, you can well have it in a sandwich as well. In this recipe, a well-seasoned chicken breast fillet is deep fried to perfection in a crunchy butter to replace burger patty and land on your sandwich.

Yield: 4

Preparation Time: 30 minutes

List of Ingredients:

- 2 pcs boneless chicken breasts, skins removed and cut into 4
- 2 teaspoons paprika
- ½ teaspoons cayenne pepper
- 2 tablespoons black pepper
- ¼ cup sugar
- Kosher salt to taste
- 4 pcs hamburger buns, toasted in butter and cut in the middle
- 8 dill pickle chips
- 2 pcs large eggs, lightly beaten
- 1 cup milk
- 1 ½ cups all-purpose flour
- 1 teaspoon baking powder
- 2 tablespoons powdered non-fat milk
- 2 qt peanut oil

ZZZZZZZZZZZZZZZZZZZZZZZZZZZZZZZZZZZZZZZZZZZZZZZZZZZZZZZ

Methods:

1. Combine sugar with some kosher salt to make a brine for your chicken breast fillets.

2. Transfer into a Ziploc bag along with chicken pieces and let sit in the fridge for 6 hours or more.

3. When chicken is ready, mix together pepper, paprika, and cayenne pepper in a bowl. Set aside.

4. Combine milk and eggs in another bowl and set aside.

5. Whisk together flour, cornstarch, milk powder, baking powder, a pinch of sugar, a pinch of salt, and 2 tablespoons of premixed spice in a large bowl until well combined.

6. Add 3 tablespoons of egg and milk mixture into the flour mixture and stir until it resembles wet sand.

7. Preheat oil in the deep fryer until its temperature reaches 350 °F.

8. Remove chicken from brine, pat dry using paper towels, and coat first with milk mixture, then the flour mixture, making sure that excess coating is shaken off.

9. Fry chicken pieces in hot oil for about 4 minutes or until crisp and brown on all sides.

10. Lay down 2 pickle chips on each bun, topped with freshly fried chicken cutlets.

11. Close sandwiches and cover with aluminum foil.

12. Let it sit for about 2 minutes and you are ready to serve.

(7) Fried Chicken Salad

Crispy fried chicken pieces are like an empty canvass. You can paint with any additional ingredients as you want to create a masterpiece. This time, we will be making fried chicken into a refreshing salad that is rich in flavors and spices. Served with buttermilk-herb dressing, this will surely impress any foodie.

Yield: 8

Preparation Time: 50 minutes

List of Ingredients:

- 8 pcs chicken breast halves, skinned and deboned
- 1 ½ cups buttermilk
- 2 tablespoons Tabasco garlic marinade
- 1 cup all-purpose flour
- 1 ¼ lbs. yellow wax beans, blanched
- 1 bunch watercress leaves, rinsed
- 1 pt grape tomatoes
- Salt and pepper to taste
- Canola oil

For the Buttermilk-Herb Dressing:

- 1 ¼ cups buttermilk
- ½ cup sour cream
- 1 tablespoon Dijon mustard
- 2 tablespoons fresh chives, coarsely chopped
- 3 tablespoons fresh basil, chopped
- 2 tablespoons parsley, chopped
- ½ teaspoons salt
- ½ teaspoons freshly ground pepper

zzzzzzzzzzzzzzzzzzzzzzzzzzzzzzzzzzzzzzzzzzzzzzzzzzzzzzz

Methods:

1. Place chicken in a Ziploc bag together with buttermilk and marinating sauce. Toss to coat meat well and place in the fridge to chill overnight.

2. When chicken is ready, preheat oil in the deep fryer until its temperature reaches 350 °F.

3. Remove chicken from the marinade and coat evenly with flour before putting into the hot oil.

4. Drain on the paper towel lined plate.

5. Meanwhile, make the sauce by mixing together buttermilk, Dijon mustard, and sour cream in a bowl. Stir in chopped herbs and season with salt and pepper.

6. Assemble salad by placing 2 lettuce leaves on a plate, topped with wax beans, fried chicken, watercress, and tomatoes.

7. Serve with buttermilk-herb dressing.

(8) Fried Chicken Steak

Serving crispy fried chicken with gravy is simply genius. The contrast of crunch and sauce would create an exciting sensation in the palate you surely would not want to miss. There is nothing different here compared to other fried chicken recipes. It's just the addition of a creamy, rich gravy that gave an amazing twist.

Yield: 6

Preparation Time: 20 minutes

List of Ingredients:

- 1 ½ lbs. chicken breast fillet, fat and skin trimmed and pounded
- 2 tablespoons butter
- 3 pcs eggs, lightly beaten
- 2 ½ cups milk, divided
- 1 ¼ cup all-purpose flour, divided
- 1 teaspoon paprika
- 1 ½ teaspoons salt, divided
- 1 ¼ teaspoons pepper, divided
- Vegetable oil for frying

zzzzzzzzzzzzzzzzzzzzzzzzzzzzzzzzzzzzzzzzzzzzzzzzzzzzzzz

Methods:

1. Place ½ cup of milk, lightly beaten eggs, and 1 cup of flour with paprika, salt, and pepper in three separate bowls. Set aside.

2. Dip meat into milk, then into seasoned flour, eggs, and again to the flour mixture to coat.

3. Preheat oil in the deep fryer until its temperature reaches 350 °F.

4. Deep fry chicken steaks for about 10 minutes or until golden brown.

5. Meanwhile, melt butter together with a tablespoon of oil in a saucepan over low fire.

6. Add 3 tablespoons of flour and stir continuously to make a roux.

7. Gradually add milk, stirring frequently to keep the bottom from burning, until thick.

8. Serve freshly fried chicken steaks with gravy and mashed potatoes. You may also add some steamed veggies on the side for a completely delightful meal.

Chapter II - Finger Lickin' Fried Food

Appetizers come in a variety of forms, but fried food almost always gets the most votes. They are suitable for any kind of party and would make delightful snacks any time of the day. From the widely popular French fries and onion rings to exquisite hors d'oeuvres like artichoke hearts and tempura, you can never go wrong with a good spread of fried finger food at the buffet table. It's finger-lickin' good, as they say.

zzzzzzzzzzzzzzzzzzzzzzzzzzzzzzzzzzzzzzzzzzzzzzzzzzz

(9) Potato Fritters

Another finger food favorite that's best when fried is the potato fritter. These bites are easy to make and very delicious to snack on. They are crispy on the outside yet soft and chewy on the inside. You may also substitute mashed potato in this recipe if you want a smoother consistency. It is definitely one of the best ways to use leftover mashed potato.

Yield: 10

Preparation Time: 30 minutes

List of Ingredients:

- 2 pcs medium-sized potatoes, peeled and grated (or 2 cups mashed potato)
- 1 pc onion, grated
- 1 pc egg, lightly beaten
- 2 Tablespoons flour
- Salt and pepper to taste
- Vegetable oil for frying

zzzzzzzzzzzzzzzzzzzzzzzzzzzzzzzzzzzzzzzzzzzzzzzzzzzzzzzzz

Methods:

1. Mix together the potatoes, onions, and egg.

2. Gradually add flour until combined with the rest of the ingredients.

3. Season with salt and pepper.

4. Preheat oil in the deep fryer until it reaches 375 °F.

5. Spoon some of the mixture out and flatten it before putting into hot oil.

6. Fry until golden brown, about 5-8 minutes.

(10) Sweet Potato Fries

One delightful twist that you can make to the usual French fries is using sweet potatoes instead of regular potatoes. The sweet difference would make you want to eat more. It's one of the best side dishes to serve with tasty burgers or grilled ham. Plus, you can alter your seasoning to go from salty to spicy to sweet. It's up to you.

Yield: 2

Preparation Time: 15 minutes

List of Ingredients:

- 3 pcs large sweet potatoes, peeled cut into ¼- x 3-inch strips
- 1 bottle vegetable oil
- Seasoning Options:
- Salt and ground black pepper
- Cinnamon and sugar
- Cajun seasoning

ZZZZZZZZZZZZZZZZZZZZZZZZZZZZZZZZZZZZZZZZZZZZZZZZZZZZ

Methods:

1. Preheat oil to 370 °F in the deep fryer.

2. Pat dry sweet potato strips with a paper towel.

3. Deep-fry fries in batches until brown and tender or about 7-10 minutes.

4. Drain excess oil by transferring cooked fries on paper towels.

5. Sprinkle with your seasoning choice and serve.

(11) Cordon Bleu Bites

This recipe features the goodness of cordon bleu and chicken nuggets in one. It is simple to make and comes out really awesome. We can't go on with this cookbook without this special dish which you can concoct for family gatherings and as part of the finger food spread to make any party memorable. Please note, though that you will be needing the oven apart from the deep fryer for this. The oven will make the cheese melt perfectly.

Yield: 6

Preparation Time: 40 minutes

List of Ingredients:

- 9 oz. lean ground chicken
- 8 oz. Swiss cheese, cut into cubes
- ¼ cup cooked ham, diced
- ½ cup breadcrumbs
- 1 pc egg, lightly beaten
- Vegetable oil

zzzzzzzzzzzzzzzzzzzzzzzzzzzzzzzzzzzzzzzzzzzzzzzzzzzzzzz

Methods:

1. Preheat oven to 350 °F.

2. Mix together the ground chicken, ham, and egg in a bowl.

3. Add the breadcrumbs carefully to make the mixture less sticky and easier to form into balls.

4. Form the bites with a cheese cube at the center.

5. Heat oil in the deep fryer until the temperature reaches 350 °F.

6. Fry cordon bleu bites for 4 minutes or until browned.

7. Transfer to a paper-towel-lined plate, then arrange in a baking pan.

8. Bake for about 20 minutes. Allow them to sit for 5 minutes before serving.

(12) Beer-y Onion Rings

The beer-infused batter makes the classic onion rings even more alluring. This recipe offers a very interesting mix of flavors. Apart from beer, there's also a pinch of paprika and dry mustard in the batter. Combine that with the sweetness of honey and you will surely never get enough of this.

Yield: 6

Preparation Time: 35 minutes

List of Ingredients:

- 2 pcs large yellow onions, cut into ½-inch slices separated into rings
- 12 oz. Lager beer
- ½ cup cornstarch
- 1 tablespoon baking powder
- 1 ¾ cups flour
- 1 tablespoon dry mustard
- 2 teaspoons of honey
- 1 ½ tablespoons paprika
- 1 tablespoon kosher salt
- Canola oil for frying

zzzzzzzzzzzzzzzzzzzzzzzzzzzzzzzzzzzzzzzzzzzzzzzzzzzzzz

Methods:

1. Combine all of the dry ingredients in a bowl.

2. Add the beer and honey. Mix until the batter becomes smooth. Allow them to sit for about 10 minutes.

3. Preheat oil in the deep fryer until its temperature reaches 375 °F.

4. Carefully dip onion rings in the batter, then fry in batches until crisp and golden brown. Each batch will take about 3 minutes.

5. Drain onion rings on paper towels and sprinkle with more salt as needed.

(13) Stuffed Peppers

A traditional Mexican dish gets a makeover when it is made into a crispy bite. The spiciness is still there but it is enhanced gracefully by a simple batter that made it ultra crunchy. This is best served with a plate of spiced rice

Yield: 4

Preparation Time: 45 minutes

List of Ingredients:

- 4 pcs chili peppers, roasted and skins, seeds, and veins removed
- ½ lb. lean ground beef
- 1 pc onion, chopped
- 2 pcs plum tomatoes, chopped
- 1 garlic clove, chopped
- 3 pcs eggs, separated
- ½ cup all-purpose flour
- 1 cup Mozzarella cheese, shredded
- Salt and pepper to taste
- Oil for frying

zzzzzzzzzzzzzzzzzzzzzzzzzzzzzzzzzzzzzzzzzzzzzzzzzzzzzz

Methods:

1. Brown ground beef in a skillet over medium fire. Stir until meat becomes crumbly.

2. Add onions, tomatoes, and garlic. Season with salt and pepper.

3. Stuff prepared peppers with a tablespoon or two of meat mixture. Fill the rest with shredded cheese. Secure slits using toothpicks.

4. Whip the egg whites until fluffy, then add the yolks and continue mixing until blended.

5. Preheat oil in the deep fryer until the temperature reaches 350 °F.

6. Coat stuffed peppers with the flour, dip in the egg, and fry in hot oil for about 5 minutes or until golden brown.

7. Drain on paper towels and serve.

(14) Mozzarella Sticks

The delicious flavor of Mozzarella cheese is further enhanced with garlic salt and breading. As you dip your teeth into the gooey, cheesy, and tasty crisps, you will definitely lose yourself.

Yield: 8

Preparation Time: 30 minutes

List of Ingredients:

- 1-16 oz. pack Mozzarella cheese sticks
- 2 pcs eggs, lightly beaten
- 2/3 cup all-purpose flour
- 1/3 cup cornstarch
- 1 ½ cups Italian breadcrumbs
- ¼ cup water
- ½ teaspoons garlic salt
- 1 qt vegetable oil, for frying

zzzzzzzzzzzzzzzzzzzzzzzzzzzzzzzzzzzzzzzzzzzzzzzzzzzzzzzzz

Methods:

1. Combine eggs with water. Set aside.

2. Mix breadcrumbs and garlic salt in another bowl. Set aside.

3. Blend in flour and cornstarch in a separate medium-sized bowl. Set aside.

4. Preheat oil in the deep fryer until it reaches 365 °F.

5. When the oil is ready, gently coat mozzarella sticks with the flour mixture, then the egg mixture, and finally, the breadcrumbs.

6. Fry the Mozzarella sticks in batches for about 30 seconds or until golden brown.

7. Drain on paper towels before serving.

(15) Crab Rangoon

Crab meat is combined with cream cheese in this excellent finger food. It's creamy and delightful, really. Wrapped in wonton wrappers for the crispy bite. One version of this recipe involves baking but nothing beats this version where you dip the crab and cream cheese wraps in hot oil.

Yield: 10

Preparation Time: 45 minutes

List of Ingredients:

- 1-14 oz. pack wonton wrappers
- 1-8 oz. pack cream cheese, softened
- 2-6 oz. cans crabmeat, drained and flaked
- ¼ teaspoons paprika
- ½ teaspoons garlic powder
- 2 Tablespoons water chestnuts, chopped
- 1 qt vegetable oil

Methods:

1. Preheat oil in the deep fryer until the temperature reaches 375 °F.

2. In a bowl, mix crabmeat and cream cheese together with paprika, garlic powder, and water chestnuts.

3. Spoon some mixture in the center of a wonton wrapper, then pinch the edges with set fingers to seal.

4. Fry wonton in batches until golden brown, about 4 minutes per batch.

(16) Shrimp Chips

Shrimp chips are a staple snack in Southeast Asia. Although it is pretty challenging to make, you can easily concoct this appetizer in your very own kitchen, with the help of an ever-helpful food processor. One thing that you must be careful when making the recipe is to be sure the shrimp is fresh.

Yield: 4

Preparation Time: 1 hour 30 minutes

List of Ingredients:

- 1 lb. shrimps, peeled and deveined
- 2 Tablespoons grated ginger
- 4 cups tapioca flour, divided
- ½ teaspoons sugar
- Salt and pepper to taste
- Canola oil, for frying

zzzzzzzzzzzzzzzzzzzzzzzzzzzzzzzzzzzzzzzzzzzzzzzzzzzzzzz

Methods:

1. Puree the shrimp and ginger in the food processor.

2. Mix 3 ¾ cups tapioca flour together with pureed shrimps in a bowl. Season with salt and freshly ground black pepper. Blend until the dough is smooth.

3. Roll the dough in a lightly floured surface, dividing it into two logs, about 7 inches long and 2 inches thick.

4. Steam shrimp logs over medium fire for about 15 minutes. Set aside in the fridge to chill until it becomes firm.

5. Slice shrimp logs into 1/8-inch thick pieces and place them on a baking sheet lined with parchment paper. Let them air dry for about 45 minutes.

6. When the shrimp chips are almost ready, preheat the oil in the deep fryer to 375 °F.

7. Deep fry chips in hot oil until they puff, about 2 minutes.

8. Transfer onto paper towels to drain excess oil.

(17) Mac & Cheese Munchies

Give your kids' favorite snack a twist by coating it in a rich batter. You will never need a spoon to bite into the cheesy goodness of classic macaroni and cheese if you use this recipe. It is as easy as counting 1-2-3.

Yield: 8

Preparation Time: 1 hour 10 minutes

List of Ingredients:

- 1-7.25 oz. package macaroni and cheese mix, cooked according to package directions
- 1 cup cheddar cheese, shredded
- 1 cup Italian cheese blend, shredded
- ¾ cup pimento cheese spread
- 2 cups Italian breadcrumbs
- 4 pcs eggs, lightly beaten
- 2 Tablespoons butter
- ½ cup milk, divided
- ½ teaspoons chili powder
- ½ teaspoons paprika
- ½ teaspoons sugar
- ¼ teaspoons salt
- ½ teaspoons ground black pepper
- Pinch of cayenne pepper
- 4 cups oil for frying

zzzzzzzzzzzzzzzzzzzzzzzzzzzzzzzzzzzzzzzzzzzzzzzzzzzzzzzzzz

Methods:

1. Combine the cooked macaroni and cheese while still hot with a ¼ cup of milk, 2 tablespoons of butter, and the cheeses. Stir until the cheeses are melted. Set aside mac and cheese in the fridge to chill and become solid for about 4 hours or more.

2. Spoon mac and cheese mixture when ready, in a parchment paper lined baking sheet. Place it in the freezer for two hours.

3. After two hours, preheat oil in the deep fryer until the temperature reaches 350 °F.

4. Mix breadcrumbs, chili powder, cayenne pepper, sugar, and pepper in a dish.

5. In a bowl, mix together eggs and milk. Season with some salt.

6. Dip each mac and cheese ball into the egg mixture, then coat in the crumb mixture before frying in hot oil for about 3-5 minutes or until golden brown.

(18) Crispy Zucchini Blossoms

If you are looking for another way to enjoy zucchini blossoms, this is the best answer. They are dipped in a delightful batter and fried to perfection, creating a satisfying and utterly addictive snack or as a prelude to any delicious main course.

Yield: 4

Preparation Time: 25 minutes

List of Ingredients:

- 2 dozen Zucchini blossoms, stamens removed
- 1 ¼ cups all-purpose flour
- 12 oz. chilled Lager beer
- 1 ½ teaspoons kosher salt, divided
- Vegetable oil

ZZZZZZZZZZZZZZZZZZZZZZZZZZZZZZZZZZZZZZZZZZZZZZZZZZZZZZ

Methods:

1. Preheat vegetable oil in the deep fryer until it reaches 350 °F.

2. Combine a teaspoon of salt with flour.

3. Add beer and mix until blended. Be careful not to over-blend the mixture so as not to deflate the batter.

4. Dip the zucchini blossoms in beer batter one-by-one, shaking off any excess. Fry in hot oil until golden brown, about 2 minutes.

5. Transfer crispy zucchini blossoms in paper towels to drain excess oil before serving.

Chapter III - Fried Sweets to Die For

Desserts are normally baked but a good lot of those you can eat as a meal finale can be deep fried as well. Check out the sweet and indulgent desserts you can use your deep fryer for in this amazing listing from cookies to ice cream and everything else in between.

ZZZZZZZZZZZZZZZZZZZZZZZZZZZZZZZZZZZZZZZZZZZZZZZZZZZZZZZ

(19) Deep Fried S'mores

This recipe is something that will make your deep fryer busy working day in and day out. That's because once your kids get a hand on these s'mores, they will keep bugging you to make more.

Yield: 12

Preparation Time: 40 minutes

List of Ingredients:

- 9 pcs graham crackers
- 20-24 pcs large marshmallows
- 2 pcs 4.25 oz. chocolate bars
- ½ cup chocolate chips
- 1 ¼ cup all-purpose flour, divided
- ½ teaspoons baking powder
- 1/8 teaspoons salt
- 3 tablespoons granulated sugar
- ¾ cup milk
- 1 pc egg
- 1 teaspoon oil
- 1 qt vegetable oil

zzzzzzzzzzzzzzzzzzzzzzzzzzzzzzzzzzzzzzzzzzzzzzzzzzzzzzzz

Methods:

1. Lay down 4 pcs graham crackers in a plastic wrap lined baking sheet.

2. Melt the chocolate chips and spread 1/3 of it onto the crackers.

3. Lay down the chocolate bars on tops of melted chocolate.

4. Top with marshmallows, then cover with the remaining graham crackers.

5. Refrigerate the s'mores to allow the chocolates to set.

6. While waiting, mix together the egg, milk, and a teaspoon of oil.

7. Whisk in flour, baking powder, sugar, and salt in another bowl.

8. Combine the wet and dry ingredients, mixing until blended and smooth.

9. Cut the s'mores into 36 squares.

10. Preheat oil until it reaches the temperature 375 °F.

11. Dip each piece into prepared batter, shaking off any excess before putting into hot oil.

12. Deep fry until golden brown or for about two minutes.

13. Dust s'mores with some powdered sugar before serving.

(20) Fried Oreos

Oreo cookies are made even more irresistible in this deep fryer recipe. You only need six ingredients and at least half an hour for this to get the most loving kisses from your kiddos.

Yield: 10

Preparation Time: 30 minutes

List of Ingredients:

- 2 qt vegetable oil
- 1 pc large egg, lightly beaten
- 1 cup milk
- 2 teaspoons vegetable oil
- 1 cup pancake mix
- 1 18 oz. pack cream-filled Oreo cookies

zzzzzzzzzzzzzzzzzzzzzzzzzzzzzzzzzzzzzzzzzzzzzzzzzzzzzz

Methods:

1. Preheat oil in the deep fryer until it reaches 375 °F.

2. In a large bowl, combine 2 teaspoons of oil, egg, and milk stirring until smooth.

3. Gradually add pancake mix until the batter is free from lumps.

4. Dip each Oreo cookie into the batter, then fry in hot oil for about 2 minutes or until golden brown.

5. Drain on paper towels and serve.

(21) Crunchy Ice Cream

Fried ice cream? This one would surely make brows raised. But it is possible. Yes, you can deep fry ice cream and maintain its delightful goodness without having to miss out on the soothing cold texture.

Yield: 4

Preparation Time: 20 mins

List of Ingredients:

- 3 cups vanilla wafer cookies
- ½ cup pecans
- 1.5 qt of vanilla ice cream, scooped onto muffin tins and frozen to become solid
- 2 cups corn flakes cereal
- 1 tablespoon of cinnamon sugar
- 2 pcs eggs, beaten
- For Garnish:
- Whipped cream
- Chocolate syrup
- Cherries

zzzzzzzzzzzzzzzzzzzzzzzzzzzzzzzzzzzzzzzzzzzzzzzzzzz

Methods:

1. Combine wafer cookies, cereal, cinnamon sugar, and pecans in a food processor. Process until it becomes fine crumbs. Transfer to a bowl.

2. Dip each scoop solid vanilla ice cream in crumbs to coat, then in egg, and then back to the crumbs.

3. Place back onto muffin tins and back to the freezer and leave overnight.

4. When you are ready to fry ice cream, preheat oil in the deep fryer until it reaches 400 °F.

5. Carefully lift twice frozen and coated vanilla ice cream and fry for a few seconds or until golden brown.

6. Garnish with whipped cream, chocolate syrup, and cherries. Serve.

(22) Orange Churros

Spain's favorite street food has spread throughout the world. In this recipe, the churros are flecked with hints of orange for an additional thrill. Plus, there's cayenne pepper for some extra kick. All of that is drowned in the goodness of hot choco syrup.

Yield: 8

Preparation Time: 1 hour 15 minutes

List of Ingredients:

- Zest and juice of 1 pc orange
- 1 ¼ cup all-purpose flour
- ¼ teaspoons salt
- 7 ½ tablespoons unsalted butter
- 3 pcs large eggs
- 4 oz. semisweet chocolate
- 1 teaspoon vanilla extract
- 3 Tablespoons water mixed with 3 tablespoons sugar
- ¼ teaspoons cayenne pepper
- ½ cup sugar mixed with ½ teaspoons ground cinnamon
- Canola oil, for frying

zzzzzzzzzzzzzzzzzzzzzzzzzzzzzzzzzzzzzzzzzzzzzzzzzzzzzzz

Methods:

1. Prepare 3 baking sheets and line them with wax paper, then, dust generously with ¼ cup of flour. Set aside.

2. Boil 1 cup of orange juice, orange zest, 6 tablespoons butter, and salt in a saucepan over medium fire.

3. Add 1 cup of flour and lower the heat, stirring constantly to form a ball.

4. Place mixture in a mixing bowl.

5. Add eggs one by one, mixing on medium speed with every addition. Continue to beat until the mixture becomes paste-like.

6. Transfer mixture onto piping bags with a ½-inch star tip.

7. Pipe heart-shaped churros onto prepared baking sheets. Allow them to sit for about 30 minutes to air dry.

8. While waiting for the churros to be ready, make the chocolate sauce by heating water and sugar mixture together with chocolates in a saucepan over low fire. Stir continuously until the mixture becomes smooth.

9. Stir in vanilla, the remaining butter, and a pinch of cayenne pepper if desired. Keep warm.

10. Preheat oil in the deep fryer until it reaches 350 °F.

11. Carefully fry churros until golden brown, about 3 minutes.

12. Coat cooked churros in cinnamon sugar. Serve with warm choco sauce.

(23) Peach, Cheese, and Nuts Wrap

A delightful mixture of peaches, Mascarpone cheese, and pecans will truly surprise you as they come together in a wonton wrapper. This recipe is a great snack alternative that will tickle your loved ones' palate. Make sure you prepare a good batch. The playful mix is simply irresistible.

Yield: 6

Preparation Time: 1 hour 5 minutes

List of Ingredients:

- 2 pcs fresh peaches, pitted and diced
- ½ cup mascarpone cheese
- 3 tablespoons salted pecans, toasted and chopped
- 25-30 pcs wonton wrappers
- 2 tablespoons sugar
- 1 pc egg, lightly beaten
- 1 tablespoon confectioners' sugar
- Vegetable oil, for frying

zzzzzzzzzzzzzzzzzzzzzzzzzzzzzzzzzzzzzzzzzzzzzzzzzzzzzz

Methods:

1. Cook peaches in a saucepan over medium fire.

2. Add sugar and stir frequently until sugar is dissolved or about 7 minutes.

3. In a bowl, mix together chopped pecans and shredded cheese.

4. Add cooked peaches and mix until well combined.

5. Preheat oil in the deep fryer until the temperature reaches 375 °F.

6. Spoon peach mixture to the center of a wonton wrapper, wash the sides with lightly beaten egg, and fold to seal tightly. Repeat with the remaining ingredients.

7. Arrange filled wontons in a damp paper-towel-lined plate, then cover with another sheet of a damp paper towel.

8. Allow to sit for 10 minutes, then fry in hot oil until golden brown or about 4 minutes.

9. Remove from oil, drain on paper towels, and transfer to a serving platter.

10. Dust with confectioners' sugar. Serve.

(24) Fried Strawberries

Fruits are best served fresh but you can also enjoy them fried. Yes, you read that right. These fried strawberries will stand as good examples. They are made even more delightful and definitely yummier when coated in a delicious batter then fried in hot oil.

Yield: 4

Preparation Time: 20 minutes

List of Ingredients:

- ½ lb. strawberries
- 1 pc egg, separated
- ½ cup all-purpose flour
- Pinch of salt
- 2/3 cup orange juice
- 1 teaspoon powdered sugar
- Vegetable oil

zzzzzzzzzzzzzzzzzzzzzzzzzzzzzzzzzzzzzzzzzzzzzzzzzzzzzzz

Methods:

1. Combine orange juice and egg yolk in a bowl.

2. Add flour and some salt and stir until combined.

3. Meanwhile, whip the egg white until stiff. Fold it into the batter.

4. Dip strawberries one by one into the batter mixture.

5. Preheat oil in the deep fryer until it reaches 350 °F.

6. Fry battered strawberries in oil and drain on paper towels.

7. Dust with powdered sugar before serving.

(25) Cheesy Pumpkin Fritters

Pumpkin fritters are made even more exciting with the addition of Parmesan cheese, making it a dessert worth indulging. It is pretty easy to make, will take only about 20 minutes to prepare, and come out utterly delicious. Kids and adults alike will surely like this, no, love this recipe.

Yield: 2

Preparation Time: 20 minutes

List of Ingredients:

- 1 ¼ cups pumpkin, shredded
- ¼ cup Parmesan cheese, shredded
- 4 tablespoons all-purpose flour
- 1 teaspoon baking powder
- 2 tablespoons milk
- 1 pc large egg
- Salt and ground black pepper to taste
- Vegetable oil for frying

zzzzzzzzzzzzzzzzzzzzzzzzzzzzzzzzzzzzzzzzzzzzzzzzzzzzzzz

Methods:

1. Preheat oil until the temperature reaches 350 °F.

2. Mix all the remaining ingredients together, making sure that everything binds well together.

3. Spoon pumpkin mixture into the deep fryer and fry them in batches until golden brown or for about 4 minutes.

4. Drain on paper towels and serve with Thai chili sauce.

(26) Jelly Doughnut Balls

Doughnuts are the most popular fried desserts there is. The trend has spun different versions and variations. As long as you have a reliable deep fryer, you can practically make any type of doughnut that you like, from the ordinary to donut fries. For this particular recipe, you will make doughnut bites. Each of these balls is stuffed with jelly spread (you can pick your favorite!) and dusted with cinnamon sugar for a truly delectable finish.

Yield: 8

Preparation Time: 2 hours 35 minutes

List of Ingredients:

- 2 ¾ cup all-purpose flour, divided
- 1 ½ cups strawberry jelly
- 1 ½ teaspoons active dry yeast, divided
- 2/3 cup warm water
- 2 tablespoons warm milk
- 1 teaspoon salt
- 3 pcs egg yolks
- 2 tablespoons butter, unsalted and melted
- 1 ¼ cup granulated sugar, divided
- Vegetable or canola oil, for frying

zzzzzzzzzzzzzzzzzzzzzzzzzzzzzzzzzzzzzzzzzzzzzzzzzzzzzz

Methods:

1. Dissolve a ¾ teaspoon of yeast in warm water.

2. Add half a cup of flour and mix until well combined.

3. Once sticky, cover the mixture with plastic wrap. Let it sit for an hour at room temperature to rise.

4. When the dough starter is ready, dissolve the remaining yeast in warm milk using a stand mixer.

5. Add butter, egg yolks, flour, 3 tablespoons of sugar, salt, and the dough starter. Continue to mix until the dough comes together.

6. Transfer dough to a lightly greased bowl, cover with cling wrap and let sit in a warm place for another hour.

7. Roll out the dough on a floured surface to ½–inch thick. Cut dough into 1-inch rounds.

8. Roll the scrap and cut out more holes to make more jelly doughnut balls.

9. Arrange the dough balls in a parchment paper lined baking pan and let sit for 15 minutes, covered with a kitchen towel.

10. Preheat oil in the deep fryer until the temperature reaches 325 °F.

11. Place strawberry jelly or your flavor of choice into a piping bag.

12. Pipe in some jelly into the dough, form into balls, and fry in hot oil until they turn golden brown or for about 2 minutes.

13. Drain excess oil from the doughnuts by transferring them onto paper towel-lined plates.

14. Once they cooled a little, coat doughnuts with the remaining sugar.

(27) Delectable Cheesecake Bites

Cheesecake is a super delicious dessert. Did you know they could be served fried and crispy? You read that right. You can enjoy cheesecakes in a bite by using this recipe.

Yield: 10

Preparation Time: 1 hour 30 minutes

List of Ingredients:

- 1-8 oz. package cream cheese, softened
- ½ cup graham cracker crumbs
- 1 teaspoon vanilla extract
- ½ cup sugar
- 1 cup all-purpose flour
- ¼ teaspoons kosher salt
- 1 teaspoon baking powder
- 1 cup whole milk
- Vegetable oil, for deep-frying

For the Strawberry Sauce:

- 1 lb. fresh strawberries, rinsed and quartered
- ¼ cup sugar
- 2 tablespoons lemon juice

zzzzzzzzzzzzzzzzzzzzzzzzzzzzzzzzzzzzzzzzzzzzzzzzzzzzzzz

Methods:

1. Prepare the cheesecake first by beating softened cream cheese until smooth, then add ¼ cup of sugar, vanilla, and graham crackers. Continue to mix until well combined.

2. Spoon cheesecake mixture balls in a wax paper lined baking sheet. Set aside in the freezer for half an hour.

3. While the cheesecake balls are freezing, make the strawberry sauce by boiling fresh strawberries, sugar, and lemon juice in a saucepan over medium fire.

4. Stir frequently to dissolve the sugar and make the strawberries release their juices or for about 7 minutes.

5. Transfer strawberry mixture to food processor or blender and puree until smooth.

6. Strain mixture using a fine mesh and set aside.

7. When the cheesecake balls are about ready, combine flour, 2 tablespoons of sugar, salt, and baking powder in a bowl.

8. Add milk and stir until batter becomes smooth.

9. Preheat oil in the deep fryer until the temperature reaches 350 °F.

10. Work with the cheesecake balls in batches, putting them onto batter to coat, before frying in hot oil for about 3 minutes or until golden brown.

11. Drain excess oil and serve with prepared strawberry sauce.

Chapter IV - Ooooh, Fried, Why Not?

There are ingredients that you are used to being served fried. But there are also those that are not quite familiar. Not that they taste bad but they are not too ordinary as fried chicken and french fries. If you are bitten by the Fry-day everyday phenomenon, you must have this listing accessible so you will not get short of cookbook ideas to pull when need be.

zzzzzzzzzzzzzzzzzzzzzzzzzzzzzzzzzzzzzzzzzzzzzzzzzzzzzz

(28) Breaded Butterflied Shrimps

This shrimp recipe will keep your loved ones happy. You can't blame them if they keep poppin' on these delectable bites one after another. The shrimps are covered in a very light batter coating so its flavors are essentially packed into every piece.

Yield: 4

Preparation Time: 35 minutes

List of Ingredients:

- 1 lb. large shrimps, peeled, deveined, and butterflied
- 1 ½ cups cornstarch
- 1 qt water
- 2 pcs eggs
- 2 cups fresh breadcrumbs
- 5 cups vegetable oil

zzzzzzzzzzzzzzzzzzzzzzzzzzzzzzzzzzzzzzzzzzzzzzzzzzzz

Methods:

1. Preheat oil in the deep fryer until its temperature reaches 350 °F.

2. Combine cornstarch, eggs, and water in a bowl, stirring until combined.

3. Dip shrimps in the batter, then coat them in breadcrumbs. Repeat the procedure again before frying the shrimps in hot oil until golden brown. Serve warm.

(29) Crunchy Pork Dumplings

Dumplings are made a lot more exciting if it is cooked in the deep fryer instead of the steamer. The addition of oil gives it a powerful punch that only the crunchy dumplings wrapper could provide. Apart from ground meat, this dish is made even tastier with bacon and napa cabbage.

Yield: 12

Preparation Time: 40 minutes

List of Ingredients:

- ½ lb. ground pork
- 1 slice bacon, chopped
- ½ cup napa cabbage, finely chopped
- 1 garlic clove, finely grated
- 1 ½ teaspoons ginger, grated
- ½ cup fresh chives, minced
- 2 pcs large eggs, divided
- ½ teaspoons sugar
- 1 teaspoon toasted sesame oil
- ½ teaspoons soy sauce
- ½ teaspoons cornstarch
- 36 pcs round dumpling wrappers, thawed
- Kosher salt
- Vegetable oil for frying
- For the Dipping Sauce:
- 3 tablespoons Ponzu sauce
- ½ teaspoons toasted sesame oil
- 1 teaspoon soy sauce
- 1 pc scallion, chopped

ZZZZZZZZZZZZZZZZZZZZZZZZZZZZZZZZZZZZZZZZZZZZZZZZZZZZZ

Methods:

1. Whisk 1 egg in a bowl.

2. Add pork, bacon, cabbage, garlic, ginger, chives, cornstarch, sesame oil, soy sauce, and sugar. Season with salt. Mix by hand until all the ingredients are well incorporated.

3. Beat the other egg in a bowl. Add a tablespoon of water.

4. Scoop dumpling filling in the middle of round wrappers. Fold and seal the edges. Arrange filled dumplings on a baking sheet and cover with a damp towel so the wrappers don't dry out.

5. Preheat oil in the deep fryer until its temperature reaches 325 °F.

6. Fry dumplings in batches for about 2 minutes or until they are crisp and golden brown.

7. To make the dipping sauce, mix together Ponzu sauce with toasted sesame oil, soy sauce, and chopped scallion.

(30) Fried Oysters

You could have oysters freshly dunk into vinegar sauce any day. But having it fried, seriously? Well, who says you couldn't? In this simple recipe, you can fry oysters perfectly using a special batter and enjoy it crunchy. You can use the same recipe for scallops and shrimps and have a crunchy food trip alright.

Yield: 4

Preparation Time: 20 minutes

List of Ingredients:

- 12 oz. oysters, shucked and drained
- 2 pcs eggs, lightly beaten
- ½ cup all-purpose flour
- ¾ cup breadcrumbs
- 1 teaspoon salt
- ½ teaspoons freshly ground black pepper
- 2 qt vegetable oil

zzzzzzzzzzzzzzzzzzzzzzzzzzzzzzzzzzzzzzzzzzzzzzzzzzzzzz

Methods:

1. Preheat oil in the deep fryer until it reaches the temperature 375 °F.

2. Place breadcrumbs in a shallow dish, beaten egg in another, and flour seasoned with salt and pepper in another.

3. Coat each oyster first in flour mixture, then egg, and finally breadcrumbs.

4. Fry in hot oil for about 2 minutes or until golden brown.

5. Transfer to a paper-towel-lined plate. Serve.

(31) Fish Tacos

Tacos are a delectable snack, which you can be tweaked to taste better, or at least, please the palate of deep-fried foodies. As a filling cod fillets are used for this recipe. Together with a bunch of spices, the fish fillets are made into crunchy filling that will surely excite your palate.

Yield: 8

Preparation Time: 1 hour

List of Ingredients:

- 1 lb. cod fillets, cut into chunks
- 1-12 oz. package corn tortillas
- ½ pc medium head cabbage, finely shredded
- 2 tablespoons cornstarch
- 1 cup all-purpose flour
- 1 teaspoon baking powder
- ½ teaspoons salt
- ½ cup mayonnaise
- ½ cup plain yogurt
- 1 cup beer
- 1 pc egg, lightly beaten
- Juice of 1 lime
- 1 teaspoon capers, minced
- 1 pc jalapeno pepper, minced
- ½ teaspoons ground cumin
- ½ teaspoons dried oregano
- 1 teaspoon ground cayenne pepper
- ½ teaspoons dried dill weed
- 1 qt oil for frying

zzzzzzzzzzzzzzzzzzzzzzzzzzzzzzzzzzzzzzzzzzzzzzzzzzzzzzzz

Methods:

1. Mix together cornstarch, flour, baking powder, and salt.

2. Combine egg and beer and immediately pour into the flour mixture.

3. Preheat oil in the deep fryer until its temperature reaches 375 °F.

4. Drench fish chunks in a bit of flour, then, dip into prepared batter, and deep fry until crispy.

5. To make the sauce, combine mayonnaise, yogurt, and lime juice, stirring until runny.

6. Add the spices and mix until well combined.

7. Lightly fry corn tortillas and lay them down on the work surface.

8. To assemble the tacos, place fried fish chunks on tortillas, top with cabbage, and drizzle with sauce.

(32) Crispy-Fried Catfish

Catfish is made into tasty crunchy bits in this recipe. It is a delight, especially for those who love hot and spicy food. Once you start popping these catfish fingers into your mouth, you will never stop munching. Catfish is abundant in Florida but you can find them available in most supermarkets. For this dish, you will need small fillets to get chicken finger like results.

Yield: 6

Preparation Time: 45 minutes

List of Ingredients:

- 3 lbs. catfish fillets
- 5 oz. Habanero hot sauce
- ½ cup buttermilk
- 2 cups all-purpose flour
- ¾ teaspoons onion powder
- 2 teaspoons salt
- ¾ teaspoons pepper
- Vegetable oil for frying

zzzzzzzzzzzzzzzzzzzzzzzzzzzzzzzzzzzzzzzzzzzzzzzzzzzzz

Methods:

1. Marinade catfish in combined buttermilk and hot sauce. Cover and chill overnight.

2. When the catfish is ready, mix together flour, onion powder, salt, and pepper.

3. Coat catfish in flour mixture, discarding marinade.

4. Preheat oil in the deep fryer until it reaches 325 °F.

5. Fry catfish in hot oil for about 8-10 minutes or until golden brown and flaky.

6. Drain on paper towels before serving.

(33) Fried Soft-Shelled Crab

Soft-shelled crabs are delicious as is but it will be even more amazing to dip your teeth into if it is cooked to a light crisp. This recipe is very easy to make you only need about five more ingredients other than the crab. In a little over half an hour, the dish could be served.

Yield: 12

Preparation Time: 40 minutes

List of Ingredients:

- 4 pcs soft-shell crabs, rinsed and cleaned thoroughly
- ½ cup milk
- 1 pc egg
- 1 cup all-purpose flour
- Salt and pepper to taste
- 4 cups vegetable oil

zzzzzzzzzzzzzzzzzzzzzzzzzzzzzzzzzzzzzzzzzzzzzzzzzzzzzz

Methods:

1. Preheat oil in the deep fryer until its temperature reaches 365 °F.

2. Place flour, seasoned with salt and pepper in a bowl, then egg and milk in another.

3. Drench each crab on flour, dip into egg mixture, and coat with seasoned flour before frying in hot oil.

4. Cook for 2 minutes or until golden brown.

5. Drain on paper towels.

(34) Deep-Fried Turkey

The all-time favorite holiday recipe gets a surprise makeover from the deep fryer. This may not be the easiest of kitchen undertakings but its result would give your palate a delectable treat. Make sure to follow the recipe closely so you will not miss out on anything and get the perfect crispy bite with a juicy inside.

Yield: 12

Preparation Time: 1 hour

List of Ingredients:

- 1 whole turkey, giblets removed and patted dry
- 4 gallons peanut oil
- Kosher salt and freshly ground black pepper

zzzzzzzzzzzzzzzzzzzzzzzzzzzzzzzzzzzzzzzzzzzzzzzzzzzzzzzzz

Methods:

1. Preheat oil in the deep fryer until its temperature reaches 350 °F.

2. Slowly lower down turkey, closely monitoring oil temperature.

3. Once the temperature drops lower, lift the turkey and wait until the temperature is 350 °F again.

4. Continue to fry until the turkey skin is golden brown and the meatiest part of the breast reads 145 °F in a food thermometer.

5. After frying, drain excess oil and sprinkle turkey with salt and pepper.

6. Let it rest for at least 10 minutes before serving.

About the Author

A native of Indianapolis, Indiana, Valeria Ray found her passion for cooking while she was studying English Literature at Oakland City University. She decided to try a cooking course with her friends and the experience changed her forever. She enrolled at the Art Institute of Indiana which offered extensive courses in the culinary Arts. Once Ray dipped her toe in the cooking world, she never looked back.

When Valeria graduated, she worked in French restaurants in the Indianapolis area until she became the head chef at one of the 5-star establishments in the area. Valeria's attention to taste and visual detail caught the eye of a local business person who expressed an interest in publishing her recipes. Valeria began her secondary career authoring cookbooks and e-books which she tackled with as much talent and gusto as her first career. Her passion for food leaps off the page of her books which have colourful anecdotes and stunning pictures of dishes she has prepared herself.

Valeria Ray lives in Indianapolis with her husband of 15 years, Tom, her daughter, Isobel and their loveable Golden Retriever, Goldy. Valeria enjoys cooking special dishes in her large, comfortable kitchen where the family gets involved in preparing meals. This successful, dynamic chef is an inspiration to culinary students and novice cooks everywhere.

Author's Afterthoughts

Thank you for Purchasing my book and taking the time to read it from front to back. I am always grateful when a reader chooses my work and I hope you enjoyed it!

With the vast selection available online, I am touched that you chose to be purchasing my work and take valuable time out of your life to read it. My hope is that you feel you made the right decision.

I very much would like to know what you thought of the book. Please take the time to write an honest and informative review on Amazon.com. Your experience and opinions will be of great benefit to me and those readers looking to make an informed choice.

With much thanks,

Valeria Ray

Printed in Great Britain
by Amazon